November and the Truffle Pig

When the old truffle sow dies, Jean-Paul has until November to turn his pet pig Pogie into a truffle hunter – otherwise she will be sent to market and might end up as pork in the but[...] But
Pogie [...] aul
is al[...] cle
whic[...] of
humo[...]

Joa[...] as
writte[...] ch
are ca[...] he

GW01607580

November and the Truffle Pig

Joan Smith

Illustrated by Janet Duchesne

Beaver Books

First published in Great Britain in 1977
by Hamish Hamilton Children's Books Limited
90 Great Russell Street, London WC1B 3PT

This paperback edition published in 1978 by
The Hamlyn Publishing Group Limited
London . New York . Sydney . Toronto
Astronaut House, Feltham, Middlesex, England

© Copyright Text Joan Smith 1977
© Copyright Illustrations on pages 13, 18, 30, 36 and 75
The Hamlyn Publishing Group Limited 1978
© Copyright remaining illustrations Janet Duchesne
1977
ISBN 0 600 36591 3

Printed in England by Cox & Wyman Limited
London, Reading and Fakenham
Set in Baskerville Monotype

All rights reserved. This book is sold subject to the condition that it shall not in any manner be lent, resold, hired or otherwise circulated without the publisher's prior consent in writing in any form of binding or cover other than that in which it is published and without a similar condition including this condition being imposed on the subsequent purchaser. No part of the book may be reproduced, stored in a retrieval system, or transmitted, in any form or by any electronic, mechanical, photocopying or recording means, or otherwise, without the publisher's prior consent in writing.

Chapter One

Unfortunately, it was already autumn when the old truffle sow died. Grandpère, sitting among the begonias on the terrace, looked doubtfully at where the young pig stood in the yard below.

'This year, it will be your turn to earn a living searching for the truffles in the wood,' he said.

Pogie, pink and portly, gazed back at him with all the understanding of a plastic plate. She could not even begin to think what might be required of her.

Jean-Paul sighed, and looked beseechingly at his grandfather. 'She's very young.'

'She's very fat. Remember, Pogie is no longer a pet. She must now earn her living with her nose in the truffle wood, like her mother before her, or she will be pork in the butcher's shop. We have no choice, Jean-Paul; we are not rich.'

'I fed Pogie every day with a bottle, and then with a tiny spoon, and it wasn't so that she would end up in slices,' said Jean-Paul severely. 'Do you remember how tiny she was, and too weak to feed with the others? She was the runt of the litter.'

'When the others went as suckling pigs to the market, she was too small to sell, so she has been eating at our expense ever since,' replied Grandpère. 'Still, it is lucky that we have her, as I did not expect to lose the old sow so soon. But you see how the leaves are already turning. It will be your task, Jean-Paul, to make Pogie into a truffle sow. You have until November.' Grandpère crossly swatted a red fly as it danced above his glass of wine. All summer he had been irritated by the flies. 'Silly, small *mouche*,' he muttered with satisfaction as it fell to the table. 'See how you are drunk with the perfume of the wine. You can no longer whizz round my head. You are easy for an old man to catch.' He swatted two more and looked better pleased.

Jean-Paul looked across the meadow to the scrubby oak wood, where the truffles grew like underground mushrooms, precious and rare, among the roots of the trees. Nowhere else in the whole of France, only here in Perigord, did a pig have such an important task to perform. It was hard on Pogie, that *she* should have been born a pig in Perigord. Jean-Paul loved her dearly, but he had never believed that she was the cleverest animal he had encountered.

He left Grandpère dozing under the vine shade of the terrace, and went down to the yard to explain more fully to Pogie. Grandmère was sitting in the doorway of the byre fattening a goose. She encouraged each in turn to feed. The maize was in a bowl, and

at intervals she measured more from a sack with a large, metal grain scoop. The bird was not particularly hungry. Pogie, who was *always* hungry, watched the process with her pale, unblinking eyes, hoping that her turn would come.

'I shall lose my temper with your Grandpère, one of these days,' said Grandmère, fiercely stroking the goose's throat, to en-

courage it to swallow. 'He will never help me with the geese, never take his turn with this work. He will sit on the terrace, drink his wine, and doze until the evening meal is steaming on the table. Not until then will he stir. One day, I will lose my temper, you see.'

'Shall I help you, Grandmère?'

'Thank you Jean-Paul, you do help often, but not now. You have the sow to train. That won't be easy.'

'Pogie,' said Jean-Paul. 'Come and start your lessons in the truffle wood. I don't think you realise how important it is that you should learn well.'

Pogie took no notice, and drooled at Grandmère as she watched the maize going down the throat of the uninterested goose. It made no sense to her. Pogie's ears, like sopping pink flannels, twitched when a fly went near. She seemed to move them deliberately to give her face a pleading expression, more like a puppy than a pig.

'That's right, Jean-Paul,' said Grandmère. 'It is important for Pogie, and it is important for me. See how fat my geese have grown already. This autumn, I shall be busy the day long, making my goose preserves. Think how pleased the fat businessman from the town will be, when he comes to buy all the little jars of potted goose. And when they contain slices of truffle, he sells them again for a *very* high price.'

'I like the preserve better without truffles, Grandmère. Truffles are just nasty black lumps.'

'Silly boy. You will learn, Jean-Paul. It is said that the flavour of one tiny slice alone is the taste of perfection. It is not for nothing, that the truffle is called the soul of Perigord. Mind you, I can't stand the taste of them myself.'

'But the fat businessman says that your goose preserve is among the best,' said Jean-Paul.

'So we must sell it to help us through the winter months,' the old woman agreed, shooing off the goose, and grabbing an-

other for its fattening feed. 'So be away, and give that Pogie of yours one useful idea in her silly, empty head.'

Jean-Paul took the long stick, with which Grandpère had always guided the old sow, to show her tactfully where she might sniff, and called to Pogie to come with him. Most farmers led their pigs on pieces of rope, but Pogie usually followed Jean-Paul around like a dog. This time, however,

Pogie was disinclined to leave Grandmère.

It was necessary to take a little of the grain from the goose's ration to tempt her away. Pogie, quick when it suited, followed him across the meadow and down to the scrubby oak wood, with sprightly enthusiasm.

The wood was scarcely worthy of that name. The poor, sandy soil and the pale stunted trees gave no clue to the wealth which lay hidden away among the twisted, knobbly roots and was waiting to be discovered by intelligent pigs.

But Pogie's first lesson was not to be private. To Jean-Paul's dismay, Monsieur

Dupont, of all people, was there, leading a pig in circles round the wood, and puffing on his pipe. For this pig was known throughout Perigord as the champion truffle sow.

Monsieur Dupont looked smug, his black smock glinting here and there, where the sun caught a greasy patch, his panama, grey and floppy with age.

'It's that *Claudine*,' said Jean-Paul to Pogie. The pig was slim and bright-eyed. Her nose, though exactly the same squat disc shape as Pogie's own, was as deep-searching as an X-ray. It was said that Claudine could read the mind of Monsieur Dupont, as if there was a nerve running through the rope by which he led her.

'Look at her,' whispered Jean-Paul. 'Look at her, Pogie, and learn where you can.' Pogie was distracted by the nodding seed head of a convenient poppy.

'By the saint of Rocamadour, young Jean-Paul, what have you got there?'

'My pig.'

'So it is. I'm sorry to hear that the old truffle sow died.'

'This is the new truffle sow,' said Jean-Paul doubtfully.

The old man nodded his head with sympathy, but could find nothing further to say on the matter. He had seen Pogie before. Pogie was making a close examination of her left foot, as if she had never noticed it until now.

'I am giving Claudine a walk round the wood to remind her that the truffles will soon be ripe in the ground, and we can seek them out. See, already she can smell them.' Claudine snorted over the sandy soil, and indicated that she would do a little digging.

'Steady on, old girl,' said Monsieur Dupont, proud and affectionate. 'They're not ready for you yet. This is free ground, Jean-Paul, so any truffles your sow can find will be yours.'

'Yes,' said Jean-Paul, brightening, feeling that perhaps the old farmer saw some hope for Pogie yet. But then he added, 'Of course, all that Claudine finds will be mine.' It was obvious from the way he spoke, that

he thought Claudine *would* find them all.

Jean-Paul said 'Pogie is very young. She has had little time to learn.'

He gently nudged her with his knee, to perk her up into a state of lively intelligence. Pogie gave him a loving stare, then rolled over on to her back, and wriggled in an ungainly way to scratch it. Jean-Paul had to help her to regain her feet. His face was red with shame. Surely, Pogie did not have to look quite so foolish in front of Claudine.

'You can tell by looking at them,' said Monsieur Dupont, shaking his head and wrinkling up his nose.

'Pogie *can* be sensible,' said Jean-Paul loyally, and glared at her.

Pogie closed her eyes as if in a sulk.

'I think,' said Monsieur Dupont, 'that to make a truffle pig out of that little joker will take a miracle. What is more, a miracle of the best quality.'

Chapter Two

The first visit to the scrubby oak wood could hardly have been called a lesson for Pogie. Jean-Paul did not feel that she could put her mind to the job on hand, when Monsieur Dupont and Claudine were stalking about the place, doing practice sniffs. He did not feel that she would be seen at her best while mastering a new skill, so he put off the actual teaching until the next day.

Fortunately, then they had the wood to themselves. They walked round for a while, Jean-Paul patiently explaining it all in simple words, and Pogie nudging his knee from time to time as if she understood. Jean-Paul indicated a likely spot with the stick.

'Try there,' he suggested.

Pogie stared at him and wondered why they had stopped.

'Sniff, like I told you. There. Big sniff.'

Pogie gazed at the spot short-sightedly with her small, pale eyes.

'Closer, and *big* sniff,' encouraged Jean-Paul.

Pogie gazed closer until her eyes crossed, like an old lady trying to thread a needle.

'Perhaps there are no truffles just there,' thought Jean-Paul, and looked for another likely spot. The trouble was, it wasn't his job to find the truffles, that was the whole point of having a truffle pig, so he could not be absolutely certain that he was asking Pogie to sniff in the right place. Of course, it was wrong to start digging until you were sure that there was a ripe truffle beneath the surface, because they were easy to damage and to waste.

'Try here, Pogie. Smell the lovely truffle. Can you smell the lovely truffle, then?'

Pogie was irritated by the bright orange flies, particularly one walking over her flank. She attempted to scratch at it with a back leg, and overbalanced. She sat down backwards, and stayed there, her mouth

open as if laughing at him.

Jean-Paul was *very* patient. On three more occasions he took Pogie to the scrubby oak wood, and repeated the lesson, each time with similar results. It did seem that some progress should be evident by this time.

'How did you start to teach the old sow, Grandpère?' asked Jean-Paul.

'Difficult to explain,' said the old man. 'I just taught her. Easy enough to do if you go about it the right way.'

'Then will you please teach Pogie, because I can't.'

Grandpère reluctantly took Pogie to the truffle wood in the late afternoon. Grandmère noted approvingly, as she looked up from the feeding of her geese. 'So he should,' she said. 'I was beginning to lose my temper with him.'

'Needn't bother with a rope,' said Grandpère. 'That pig follows you like a dog. That's half her trouble I should think, too much of a pet she is.'

Pogie was delighted to have the company of Grandpère, and danced to the wood ahead of them.

'Come here, Pogie,' called Grandpère. Pogie trotted skittishly off in the opposite direction.

'Stupid animal,' said Grandpère, going after her. Pogie waltzed back round an oak tree.

'Come *here*,' he bellowed. Pogie showed her appreciation of the game by including a fancy step or two, as she circled Jean-Paul, and pretended that she was making for home.

It took half an hour to catch her, and eventually, Grandpère held her firmly by the ear. 'Now get on with it,' he said.

Pogie used her ears to give expression to her feelings. 'I really can't,' she seemed to say, and lay down heavily in the shade of the hedge.

'She's tired, poor thing,' explained Jean-Paul.

'*She's* tired,' said Grandpère in exasperation. 'Take her home.'

It took a further half hour to lure Pogie back to the yard.

'That sow has too many problems,' said Grandpère. 'She has nostrils of cement. All

that a pig must do is learn the scent. But with this Pogie, a truffle is as safe as garlic in a tin. I'll take her to market as soon as she is a little heavier.'

'Give her a bit longer, Grandpère, *please*. I'm certain I can train her.'

'A good sow should not need all this fuss. I'll give you until November, and that will be that, Jean-Paul.'

Pogie was relaxing in the yard. Jean-Paul sat beside her and stroked her ears, hoping he had not sounded cross with her in the wood. Suddenly, he realised what had been the trouble.

'Of course, Pogie, you don't know what you're looking for, do you?'

'No,' said Pogie by flapping one ear over her eye. It was all so obvious now.

'So the answer, quite simply, is to get hold of a bit of truffle. It will have to be a bit of last year's crop, so that we can have time to practise before the truffles in the wood are quite ready, or *that* Claudine will have sniffed them all out before you've got the idea of what to do.'

Pogie closed her eyes and looked happy.

'You poor little dear,' whispered Jean-Paul. 'How could you possibly have learned the scent? We were most unfair to you.'

Pogie grunted and fell contentedly asleep in the evening sun.

Jean-Paul went into the kitchen and found Grandmère skinning a rabbit for the evening meal. The stock pot bubbled in the dark kitchen, and Jean-Paul knew that there would be two delicious meals from one rabbit, one with the herbs, one with the leeks which were lying in an untidy bunch on the table. Grandmère was usually in her best mood when preparing food.

'Have you, by any chance, a small pot of preserved goose left over from last year, or perhaps a jar of pâté? The very smallest

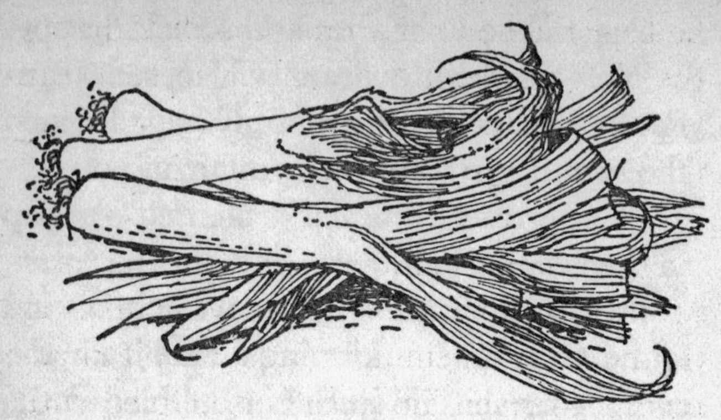

of course, with just a tiny piece of truffle in it?'

'What a question, Jean-Paul. By the saint of Rocamadour, should we be living like Lords? We eat the special pâté once a year only, on the day that the fat businessman takes away my little pots and pays us in return. We eat the last scrapings of the basins to celebrate. What a silly question, boy.'

Jean-Paul nodded, and went out of the kitchen to his bedroom. All the bedrooms led off the kitchen, and in each lingered the familiar, comforting smell of simmering stock. In the bottom of his clothes cupboard, he kept the bowl of a broken milk ladle. In the bowl, he kept his money. He liked the way the francs chinked against the metal of the bowl, it made the amount he had sound excitingly greater.

Some of the money he had earned from Monsieur Dupont for hoeing vegetables in the heat of the summer, and once Grand-mère had given him some for helping with the geese. He was going to buy a new reel

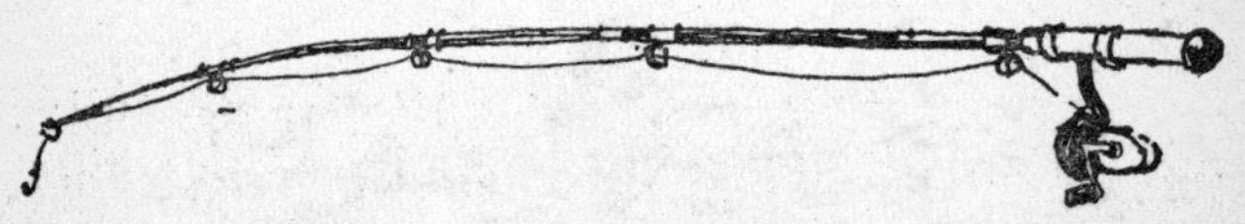

for his fishing rod, and he wanted to buy it soon, because in the new year, the fish in the river would be spawning, and he would not be able to make use of the reel until summer.

He had seven francs, and he realised that the truffle pâté in tins which you could buy in the town would be very expensive, and would take most of this. But he was prepared to sacrifice the new reel if he could save Pogie, and teach her to be a real truffle sow.

'I think I'll come with you,' he said, the next time that Grandpère announced he was going to the town with some chickens. 'I might look at the fishing reels in the shops.'

In the cart he was very quiet, because he could not help thinking that perhaps on its next trip to the town, the cart would be

carrying Pogie on her way to the market. November was not far away.

While Grandpère was talking to his friends, Jean-Paul slipped off to a rather expensive shop, where he knew that truffle pâté was sold in tins.

He chose the smallest, and hoped that it was one which contained more than its fair share of truffle. Even this small one cost six francs and twenty centimes. Being such a small tin, it was easy to conceal beneath his jersey during the journey home. Grandpère would not approve at all of this idea.

The next morning, Jean-Paul made certain that he and Pogie would be alone in the scrubby oak wood. He had opened the tin previously in the kitchen, put the pâté in a bag, and thoroughly hidden the tell-tale tin in the rubbish bucket.

Very carefully, he dug three small holes in various parts of the wood, and in each put a quarter of the truffle pâté, covering the expensive treasure with a thin film only of sandy soil, to make the sniffing easy. He did not try to prevent Pogie from seeing what he was doing, because Pogie could do with all the help she could get.

'Now you can eat this piece that is left,' he said. 'It's to get you interested, because now you will really know what you are looking for. There will be no excuse. The juices inside your mouth will all start running for truffles, and you'll be off like a bonfire in the wind to hunt for them. You see.'

Pogie obligingly ate the truffle pâté, because she ate everything anyway. But she didn't move. She did not start sniffing wildly at the ground.

'That pâté cost more than six francs,' Jean-Paul reminded her.

With a sinking heart, he led her round the wood and pointed to the places where the pâté was buried. Pogie was as casual as ever, and did not offer to sniff even once.

Jean-Paul licked his finger, where a sliver of truffle stuck to it, like a black diamond.

'You're right, Pogie. It doesn't taste of anything. Not a bit like Grandmère's truffle pâté anyway. That's the first sign of sense you have ever shown, Pogie.'

But as they walked home, the tears splashed fast down Jean-Paul's face. He cried at first for his fishing reel money, lost for sticky lumps of truffle buried in the sandy soil of the scrubby oak wood. Then he cried for the pâté which might once have been as beautiful as that made by Grand-mère, because now its delicacy was gone, its special flavour driven away, all because of trying to imprison its perfection within a metal can. For a moment he was glad they were poor, because they could taste perfection just one evening in the year.

Chapter Three

When they got home, Grandpère was relaxing on the terrace beneath the canopy of vines, idly swatting, from time to time, the flies which had big green wings. Grandmère could be heard muttering from within the kitchen, from which room came the rich smell of a stew with garlic. Jean-Paul was sadly remembering, and agreeing with, the words of Monsieur Dupont, that only a miracle could make a truffle sow out of Pogie. A miracle of the best quality he had said. But suddenly the words had a helpful meaning.

'Grandpère,' he began. 'It *is* true, isn't it, that the statue at the shrine of St Rocamadour can perform miracles?'

'A load of make-believe, my boy, is that story, encouraged as a legend in order to make money out of the summer visitors.' Grandpère took off his hat, scored over a

persistent greenwinged insect, and grunted as he mopped up the wine he had spilled in the effort.

'But the relics of the saint himself are buried there, giving great powers. It has always been so.'

'That is the most popular of the fairy tales,' agreed the old man reluctantly.

'And when a miracle happens, the bell of the chapel rings out of its own accord to proclaim the event,' persisted Jean-Paul. 'It has happened over hundreds of years.'

'But the bell seems to have abandoned the habit of late,' Grandpère pointed out. 'I have heard of no miracles, either.'

Jean-Paul nodded, and went into the kitchen where he hoped to find a more sympathetic ear. 'I know there hasn't been a miracle at Rocamadour for centuries,' he said sadly to Grandmère. 'So I suppose they never really happened?' He looked hopefully at the old woman, as she carefully wiped the pan in which she had fried the potatoes. She began to ladle out the stew.

'Each must believe what he must,' said Grandmère gently, noting the expression on Jean-Paul's face. 'But remember, we each have more to do with making our own miracles than we realise.'

Jean-Paul watched his grandfather come into the kitchen, attracted by the smell of the meal. The wine glass was safe now from the green-winged insects. It was the quiet note of hope in Grandmère's words that made Jean-Paul resolve to go to the chapel of Rocamadour the very next day, and ask for a miracle on behalf of Pogie. It would be the very last attempt he could make.

Rocamadour was only one kilometre away, but with the reluctant Pogie walking beside him, the way seemed much further.

'See, the leaves are all yellow and bronze, Pogie. When they have fallen, it will be November.'

Pogie tried to sit down.

'Get up. We're doing this for you. We want to be there at the time the priest will

be taking his meal, and perhaps a quick nap afterwards. So come along.'

A leaf fell, gentle as drifting bonfire ash, and Jean-Paul quickened his step.

Rocamadour was before them, a tiny village clinging like a barnacle to the side of a steep hill. It appeared to be built one house on top of another.

'We've got the steps to come yet,' said Jean-Paul. The thought of getting Pogie up the two hundred steps that led to the chapel built high over the village was beginning to worry him. But if Pogie was to be the subject of a miracle, it would be a lot easier for the saint if Pogie was to hand. Jean-Paul was hazy as to the strength of miracle power over long distances.

The main street was quiet. The women had finished buying in the market, and were at home preparing vegetables for the midday meal. The shop owners were closing their doors. Jean-Paul had his sandwich with him, half a long loaf, split and filled with slices of sausage. But he preferred to accomplish his task satisfactorily before

eating. Very few people stared at the boy and the pig walking though the village street.

A few more people stopped to stare at the sight of Pogie climbing the steps which led to the chapel high on the hillside. After the first twenty, Pogie showed her disapproval by turning round and starting to go down again. Fortunately, Jean-Paul had thought to put a rope on her, and not rely as he usually did, on her inclination to follow him everywhere. With a sharp tug he stopped her, and then with considerable pushing and gentle persuasion, managed to get her pointing in the right direction once more.

'The ancient pilgrims coming to the shrine climbed all these steps on their knees,' said Jean-Paul severely. 'That was a great deal harder. It was a sign of

humility. No wonder miracles happened for them. You don't get miracles to happen by being lazy, Pogie.'

Pogie did not seem a bit humble, she was more outraged than pleading, and very lazy indeed about getting up the steps. By the time the two had reached the chapel, Jean-Paul began to worry that the priest would have returned from his lunch.

Outside the chapel, there were some boxes of candles. You could buy one and burn it within the church. They were priced at one franc for a small thin one, and there were others, thicker and better, for four francs.

'We ought to buy a candle, Pogie, if we're asking favours, but I've only got eighty centimes left. I could have afforded one if we hadn't bought that tin of truffle pâté. Never mind, it's the thought that counts. I hope. Let's go inside.'

The door of the chapel stood half open, and even from the outside, Jean-Paul could feel the cool within, cool which never changed, like a cave, or a deep part of the sea.

Cautiously, he glanced round him. No-one was looking.

'Now,' he said, and gave Pogie a push through the door. Pogie didn't like the cold, much preferring sun warmth on her back. Neither did she like the dark, her pale eyes did not accustom themselves quickly. Annoyed, Pogie charged ahead and blindly crashed through a row of chairs.

'This is no way to get a miracle, you stupid creature. No-one will help a bad-tempered pig. You must look humble and

pathetic.' Pogie crossly nudged over another chair.

Jean-Paul managed to sit her quietly on the floor at the back of the tiny chapel, and leave her while he rearranged the seats in their original positions.

'My son,' said a quiet, gentle voice behind him. 'You must also replace the pig on the outside of the church.'

Jean-Paul looked round, startled. A priest was watching him, very kindly, but clearly very firm.

'I had to bring her in, because I want a miracle done on her,' he explained. 'And we've come up all those steps.'

'But surely you see we can have no pigs in this house,' said the priest. He was so kind, so polite, that to argue was out of the question.

'I'll put her outside, while I ask,' said Jean-Paul. 'I just hope she doesn't run away or get into trouble.'

'Perhaps I could hold the rope, then you will know she is safe,' suggested the priest.

'Thank you,' said Jean-Paul. 'I was hoping you might.'

The priest looked worried. 'You are not believing *too* much that the chapel bell will ring for you? Not *relying* on it, I hope, because the bell disappoints many these days.'

'I want to try,' said Jean-Paul.

'Of course, my son, of course. Anyone may ask at the altar.'

Jean-Paul took Pogie out of the chapel, and returned alone, leaving the sow and the priest contemplating each other suspiciously, at either end of the rope. Jean-Paul walked to the altar with his head bowed, knelt on

the stone step before the rail, and looked up slowly, wearing his most beseeching expression.

The famous statue was truly disappointing. She was very small and did not look important enough for a shrine where the bones of a saint were buried. On top of that, she was surprisingly *sooty*, quite black in parts. She was not a black African lady

Virgin, like a picture Jean-Paul had seen in a new school scripture book, but an ordinary French one, gone discoloured.

'It's because you're so ancient,' said Jean-Paul consolingly.

He was staring at her, trying to decide how best to introduce the subject of miracles, when he noticed her expression.

It was not pure and holy, like the statue in the church at home, and it was not gentle and understanding like the little one Grand-mère kept in her bedroom. Nor was it

disapproving like the one in the cathedral in the town.

This one was amused. She was full of fun, almost looking as if she had enjoyed seeing Pogie knock the chairs over.

Jean-Paul grinned back. He felt a great sense of relief. Here was a statue capable of understanding the situation.

He bowed his head and tried to put the case for a miracle as clearly as possible, adding as an afterthought, 'Pogie *didn't* like those steps, you know, and I helped with the geese twice last week without being asked. And remember, I haven't put pepper on the goat's beard since last Easter.'

When he could think of nothing else to say, he raised his head once more, as if seeking an answer.

The amused expression had not left the face of the statue, and Jean-Paul felt a deep, warm certainty within himself that his request had been heard, and that a solution would be forthcoming.

He did not know quite how to take his leave, so he looked round to see if he could

see the bell, the one which rang of its own accord when a miracle occurred.

He discovered it hanging in the roof, a most unusual-looking bell. The metal was pitted and uneven, dull with age. The clapper was frail and tinged with rust. It was many centuries old.

'Ding. Dong,' said Jean-Paul, dropping a little hint, and he could well imagine the sound that such a bell would make. Most unmusical he was sure, not much of a chime by today's standards.

There was a shout and a clatter outside. Jean-Paul turned round to see Pogie peeping inquiringly round the door. She looked full of innocence, being jerked at intervals as an irate priest tried to prevent her entering the chapel. Pogie was unmoved.

'*That's* Pogie, see,' Jean-Paul said hurriedly, before rising to his feet. 'Oh, and it *will* be a miracle of the best quality, won't it? Nothing half-hearted would work on Pogie.'

Above him, the smile on the face of the statue seemed to deepen. For a moment she might have been about to give him a cheeky wink.

'Thanks,' said Jean-Paul and rushed hastily to the door, to rescue either Pogie or the priest, whoever should have the greater need.

Chapter Four

Jean-Paul went home happy. Pogie went home, still reluctant and oblivious of the wonderful change that was about to overtake her. She disliked descending the steps even more than she disliked going up them. Jean-Paul had to tempt her with pieces of bread from his sandwich, but he ate the sausage himself, as he felt that would be an unkind reminder of the fate which had been hanging over her head.

'Just think, Pogie, how much slimmer you will be after today's exercise. Grand-père won't be in a hurry to take you to market, which is a good thing in case the miracle takes a lot of time to come about.'

They ambled back to the village, Pogie nibbling at the corn if ever she had a chance. 'The miracle is as good as done,' said Jean-Paul. 'That statue was really great, she understood everything I said,

even seemed to think it was a bit of a joke. The only question is, when will it be? I expect you will be a slow subject, Pogie, and of course a best quality miracle will take longer than an everyday one.'

The following morning started misty, and turned into yet another perfect autumn day. 'These *mouches* will dance for ever,' said Grandpère, grabbing a blue-ringed insect with his fingers. It was while Jean-Paul was admiring the branches as they lost their leaves, and were beginning to resemble black lace against the sky, that he saw Monsieur Dupont take Claudine to the truffle wood.

With her delicate, aristocratic nose, she discovered the first truffle of the season, as large as a fist, black and wrinkled but firm within, mature and absolutely perfect. It lay in the far corner of the wood. Monsieur Dupont dug it up with his gleaming, metal truffle digger, and placed it lovingly in his rush basket. He and Claudine continued this work throughout the morning, and the brilliant pig gave not one false sniff.

At midday, the old man joined Grand-père in a glass of wine. 'This will be a fine

year for truffles,' he said. 'There will be more than we need for our good women to flavour the pâté and the goose preserve. We can sell them whole. Some call them black diamonds, and the price they will fetch will make us believe they are really jewels.' He laughed and emptied his glass.

'When will you take Pogie to the wood?' he asked Jean-Paul.

'Tomorrow.'

'Then we can work together. Tomorrow, I will take Claudine there again. We shall see if Pogie has grown into a truffle sow.'

'I have just remembered,' said Jean-Paul quickly, 'that I promised Grandmère I would fetch more grain for the geese from the market tomorrow.'

'That's kind of you, Jean-Paul. I thought I had to go myself,' said Grandpère, and had every intention of keeping him to that promise, which was almost certainly not yet made.

'This afternoon, I mend my byre,' said Monsieur Dupont. 'So first I must go to the town to obtain good timber.'

'Ah,' said Jean-Paul. 'Pogie and I will be truffle-hunting this afternoon. I had forgotten that is what I had planned to do.'

'The truffles will be there for many weeks. There for the finding. But I hope your Pogie is accurate. You must remember not to disturb the earth unnecessarily.'

'I know that,' said Jean-Paul quietly, visualising little piles of earth where Pogie's search had been fruitless. But it would be something, if only she would sniff.

Monsieur Dupont departed on his errand. The autumn sunshine twinkled on his bald head as he waved his floppy hat. He was a happy man, his sow was rewarding him well.

'Tomorrow is the first day of November,' said Grandpère. 'The sow should go to market, though she is not as fat as I had expected.'

'Give her a little more time,' pleaded Jean-Paul. 'You did say November, not the very first day of it.'

'Tomorrow,' said Grandpère firmly. 'How I wish the old sow had not died before the truffle time, or even that we could afford a new one. As it is, we only have Pogie.' He sighed and half-heartedly hit out at a large black fly.

Jean-Paul joined Grandmère in the kitchen where she was ladling out potato soup.

'Grandmère, I'm sure that Pogie will find some truffles. But just supposing she doesn't, what will we do?'

'I will buy some from Monsieur Dupont,

and that will take half my profit. We deserve the money we make Jean-Paul, it is hard work with the geese.'

'I'm sure Pogie will succeed.'

'How can you be so sure? She has given us no reason for thinking so. Your Grandpère should have trained her beside the old sow of course. But he didn't. I suppose he is sitting out there now, drinking in the sunshine?'

'He was talking with Monsieur Dupont.'

'Aah, yes. I will lose my temper with your Grandpère quite soon I believe.' She threw the soup into the bowls with her ladle, so that it splashed on to the checked table cloth. 'Pah,' she said. 'My temper is close to an explosion.'

After the meal, Jean-Paul and Pogie walked across the field to where the scrubby oak trees grew. He led her on a rope to make her feel more professional. He looked unhappily at the filtering shafts of winter sunshine, for they grew wider each day as the leaves fell. In the still brightness, small yellow insects relentlessly danced.

'Pogie,' said Jean-Paul severely. 'November will be here tomorrow. This is your last chance. I have done everything I can think of, to help you. Even *you* tried, by climbing the steps at Rocamadour, but you messed up that attempt by knocking over the chairs in the chapel. Not respectful, was it? No wonder we are being kept waiting for the miracle. All you have to do is learn the *smell* of the truffle. It is there all the time, waiting for you, hanging in the air. Please, Pogie, really *try* this time. I'd dig myself, if I thought it would do any good.'

Together they walked round the wood, Jean-Paul indicating with a stick from time to time, the most promising-looking areas. Pogie dutifully looked at each spot until her eyes crossed. Then Jean Paul pressed the flat disc of her nose to the ground, Pogie did a huge sniff to get air, filled her nostrils with soil, and spent the next five minutes in a sneezing fit.

Jean-Paul thought hard about the statue in the chapel at Rocamadour. 'You haven't forgotten, have you?' he whispered.

'Because I know you heard, I *know* you did.'

Pogie gave a little sniff at the ground on her own account, to see what had caused the sneezing.

'Good *girl*,' said Jean-Paul, putting all his energy into encouraging praise. 'Again. Again.' He took huge sniffs at the air to demonstrate. The statue could not complain of lack of enthusiasm, he was with her all the way.

Pogie found something which interested her, and steered a course like a whippet after an electric hare, straight between two oak saplings, growing only a foot apart.

Pogie's triangular head went through the gap, her broad strong shoulders followed, propelled by the speed at which she was moving. But then she ran out of steam.

She was wedged between the saplings, like a finger in a tight ring. In front, her pink flannel ears flopped over her eyes with disbelief. Behind, her back legs scrabbled ineffectively against the sandy soil.

'Are *you* really *trying*?' asked Jean-Paul, facing in the direction of Rocamadour. He turned back to Pogie. 'I had hoped for a clever pig when I fed you twice a day, and woke in the night to do so as well,' he said severely. 'I had not hoped to rear a pig with the brain of a fly. A *mouche*. An over-sized Pogie *mouche* is what you are.'

'Please,' said Pogie with her ears, pawing at the ground feebly, to show what a frail creature she truly was.

After a certain amount of fruitless pushing and pulling, Jean-Paul eventually freed the sow by tying her leading rope round one of the two saplings. He was now able to bend it away from her, relieve the pressure, and allow Pogie to push her way through to freedom. Even then, he had to give her a gentle kick on the back end to indicate that she was free to move.

'It's no use, Pogie,' said Jean-Paul. 'I have been mistaken. We might as well go home. I'm sorry I was unkind.' He could feel the tears of frustration gathering in his eyes.

Pogie nudged him with her round, smooth nose, and her pale eyes gave a rewarding though brief gleam of affection.

He put his arm round her broad back, and they walked sadly through the wood.

At first, only half-heartedly, did he notice the behaviour of the flies.

But then he realised something and stood quite still, looking round with excitement thumping in his chest.

Chapter Five

The small yellow insects hung in columns, like lanterns. They danced here and there, but not everywhere. Mostly they moved up and down in a pattern, but a few tumbled and whirled without reason, much as they did over Grandpère's wine glass.

At first, Jean-Paul had wondered why. By the time he had sniffed the tears from his eyes, he knew. He took a quick glance round. It was necessary that he should have a little dig. But he knew that he had good reason to do so. His faith in Pogie had been such that he had not brought a digging tool with him, so he had to use a twig.

He approached the spot over which the nearest column of insects danced, and then cautiously scratched the surface of the earth. He searched just a little deeper.

He hardly dare believe his eyes. There, like a black diamond, lay a small but perfect truffle. The yellow flies had been dancing precisely over it, and had become drowsy with the delicate perfume.

Jean-Paul showed his find to Pogie. She inspected it obediently, crossing her eyes until the smell caught her nostrils. She sniffed. She looked at Jean-Paul and then she sniffed again. Her pale eyes filled with ecstasy. She sniffed, she routed in the leaves, she danced with excitement. She came alive.

'Pogie, I think you're going to be a truffle sow. We've been so wrong about you. You're not a Pogie-*mouche*. It is only that you don't waste your time, sniffing after this and that among the leaves. You've been saving yourself for the truffles.'

Pogie closed her eyes with modest agreement.

'Now, you must find a truffle all on your

own. Let's try over there under some more flies. Just take a little help from them to begin with.'

Pogie was reluctant to leave the first truffle, believing it to be the only one of its kind. She watched it lingeringly as Jean-Paul dragged her away, and was amazed to find another at the next spot that he indicated. She would have preferred him, and not her, to have done the digging to uncover it.

'This time, you must do everything yourself.' Jean-Paul dragged her to a fresh part of the wood. Pogie looked at him and waited to be shown where to find the next delight. Jean-Paul looked at Pogie and did absolutely nothing except cross his fingers behind his back.

Pogie looked round. She sniffed the air and was disappointed. She put the flat disc of her nose to the ground and got a hint. She moved a little further on, to where the perfume became stronger, she scraped with her foot, and this time discovered entirely on her own, that there was a truffle lurking close beneath the surface.

She lifted her head and started sniffing again.

'Steady on, Pogie, you're going wild.'

Through the trees, Jean-Paul saw Grandpère come out of the house, so he ran to the edge of the wood and called 'Grandpère, fetch the baskets. Pogie is truffle hunting.'

'What?' Grandpère was growing deaf, and Jean-Paul did not have a loud voice. He had to run halfway across the field before his Grandfather understood.

The old man held up his hand. 'I'll fetch the baskets,' he said, and turned back into the house.

Jean-Paul watched him disappear and was about to return to the scrubby oak wood. Pogie would be tossing up truffles like chestnuts cracking on a fire.

But he was stopped in mid turn by the sound of dull metal ringing unmusically against its own kind. The sound was clear in the field.

It could only be the ancient bell of Rocamadour proclaiming a miracle.

He had forgotten the bell in his excitement when Pogie found the truffle, forgotten about the miracle altogether. What else could sound like that, but the rusty clapper against the pitted bell? It was exactly as he had imagined.

Again it rang out, and for a third time, before falling silent. How strong the miracle must be that the bell should ring so loud and the sound be heard so far from Rocamadour.

He could not see the village on the hillside, but he could imagine its people running like ants to listen to the bell ring out, the bell which had not sounded of its own accord for centuries. Tonight they

would discuss what the miracle might have been. But only he, Jean-Paul, knew that.

'Thank you,' said Jean-Paul. 'I knew you had listened to me. I knew when I saw you smiling. I thought you liked a joke, and that's why you kept us waiting until the last moment.' He knew that she would want him to appreciate that, though personally he thought it rather a feeble joke.

Grandpère was a long time finding the baskets. When he finally appeared walking across the field, he was rubbing his shoulder, carrying two baskets in one hand.

'*I* would have thought of something not quite so feeble,' Jean-Paul thought.

'Your Grandmère lost her temper,' said the old man.

'She did promise that she would soon.'

'But for the wrong reason. She thought I had returned to the house to sit on the terrace once more. In fact, I had returned only to assist with collecting the truffles for the good woman herself.' Grandpère looked hurt and outraged by the unfairness of the situation.

'The truffles will please her,' consoled Jean-Paul.

'When we have collected them, I might return to the house and offer to feed the geese this evening. It will give your Grandmère a pleasant rest.'

'Whatever did Grandmère say to you when she lost her temper? You've never offered to help with the geese before.'

'She did not say a single word.'

'Whatever happened then?'

'First, she threw the grain scoop at me and it hit the frying pan. Then she threw the milk ladle and that hit the stew pot. Finally, she hit me with the milking stool

and I fell against the churn. She can be a very noisy lady, your Grandmère, when roused.'

Jean-Paul said nothing.

'But at least we can be pleased that Pogie has discovered a talent for the truffles at last. That should put her in a better mood.'

'Pogie is going wild, searching for them.'

'Like I said, you see, they only have to learn the scent. There is hardly any further training. Who knows, Pogie might be better than Claudine. Our Pogie, the Queen of Perigord.'

'You'll be amazed when you see her,' said Jean-Paul. 'She has probably unearthed half the truffles in the wood by now.

That's funny, where is she? I can't see her working.'

The wood appeared empty. Nowhere could they see the round pink back skipping from truffle to truffle, neither could they hear her snorting gently under the leaves.

'See all those yellow insects?' asked Grand-père. 'Would you believe they are called truffle flies?'

'Yes,' said Jean-Paul. 'And we know why. But I can't see any of the truffles that Pogie has dug up either.'

'No Pogie and no truffles,' agreed Grand-père.

'Odd,' said Jean-Paul. 'That is where we found the first one.'

'Nothing there now.'

When they did find Pogie, Jean-Paul turned thoughtfully to look in the direction of Rocamadour once more.

Pogie lay under an oak tree dozing contentedly on her side. She was grinning as happily as the statue herself, and on her nose were the last black crumbs of the truffles she had discovered.

'It's no good if she eats them, is it?' said Jean-Paul, aghast.

'You've taken the rope from her neck. Did you think that was to lead her *to* them?'

'I thought she needed leading.'

'Tomorrow, you will use it to lead her away, and the truffles won't be lost,' Grandpère chuckled.

Jean-Paul looked affectionately at the sleeping Pogie, it seemed ungracious to wake her. He understood now why the black statue had smiled so, as she looked down at him in Rocamadour. He should have known she wouldn't play a feeble joke.

We hope you have enjoyed this Beaver Book. Here are some of the other titles:

The Adventures of Nicholas and the Gang Whether they are having their photographs taken at school or playing cowboys and Indians in the garden Nicholas and his friends just can't keep out of trouble! A collection of hilarious stories by René Goscinny; illustrated by Sempé

Exploring Nature A Beaver original. Make earthworms come at your command, learn the secret of the oak gall and discover how a fairy ring grows – just a few of the many exciting projects in this book for the budding naturalist. Written by Derek Hall and illustrated by Tony Morris

The Mixture as Before A bumper collection of stories and limericks full of lovable and amusing characters. Written and illustrated by Charlotte Hough for younger readers or for reading aloud

Patchwork Mystery When Joe's grandmother disappears, the discovery of a crazy patchwork elephant leads him on his final, hopeful search for her. Set in Australia, this is a realistic and exciting story for six- to nine-year-olds by Nance Donkin

The Rubber Band Book A Beaver original. Tricks and puzzles to amaze your friends, games to play and toys to make – all using rubber bands – abound in this fun-filled book by Eric Kenneway, with amusing illustrations by Alan Rogers

New Beavers are published every month and if you would like the *Beaver Bulletin* – which gives all the details – please send a large stamped addressed envelope to:

Beaver Bulletin
The Hamlyn Group
Astronaut House
Feltham
Middlesex TW14 9AR

365913